Finger Painti...

11 Colorful Early Elementary Piano Solos with Optional Teacher Accompaniments

Dennis Alexander

MW01152794

This series of books is designed to provide piano students with a wide variety of musical repertoire to enhance reading and performance skills and serve as a basis for subsequent musical studies. This first book contains eleven short solos in numerous 5-finger patterns. The student is introduced to basic elements of notation, and the tuneful melodies are divided between the hands.

For added motivation and enjoyment, optional teacher accompaniments have been included. As a child, I was always very inspired when my teacher performed with me. I know now that these early musical experiences provided the basis for a lifetime of enjoyment playing ensemble music and at the same time developed secure rhythm and reading skills.

The many moods expressed in this volume will encourage young players to use their musical imagination. I hope that these pieces provide many hours of enjoyment and inspiration for both you and your students!

Dennis Alexander

Ancient Dance 18

Chocolate Fudge Swirls 12

Giggle Bugs 4

Happy Holiday! 16

Hip Hop 8

Lazy, Hazy Day, A 22

Moonfinder 2

Peaceful Peach 20

Pepperoni March 6

Sad Warrior, The 10

Sunday Swing 14

This collection is dedicated to my friend and colleague Cheri Dyer.

Illustrations: Tom Gerou
Cover art courtesy of PhotoDisc

Moonfinder

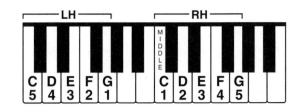

Dennis Alexander

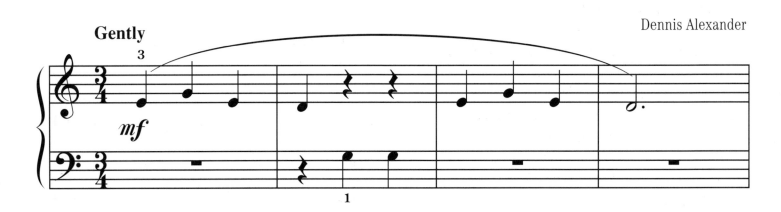

OPTIONAL DUET PART: (Student plays one octave higher.)

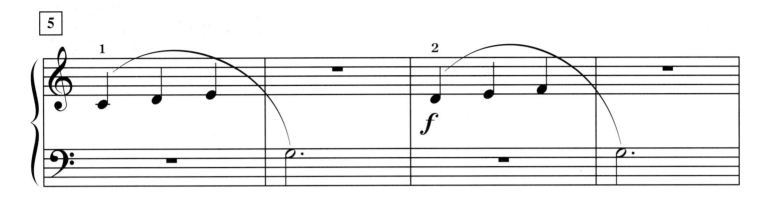

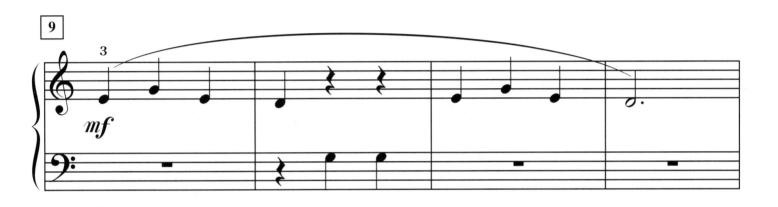

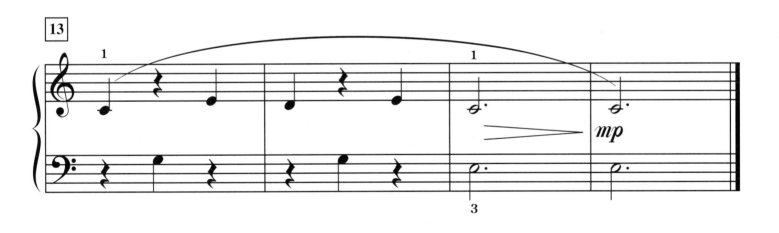

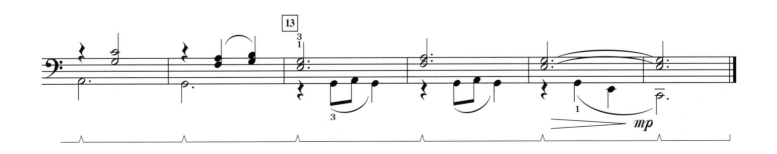

Giggle Bugs

Dennis Alexander

Giggly!

OPTIONAL DUET PART: (Student plays one octave higher.)

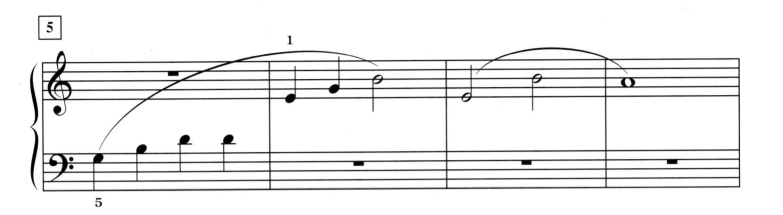

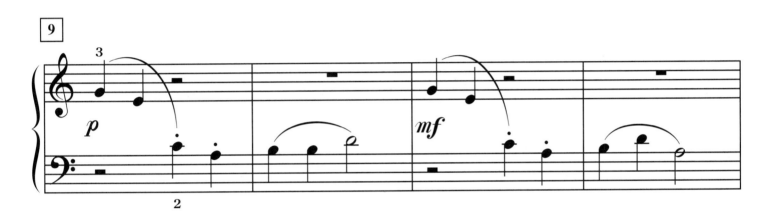

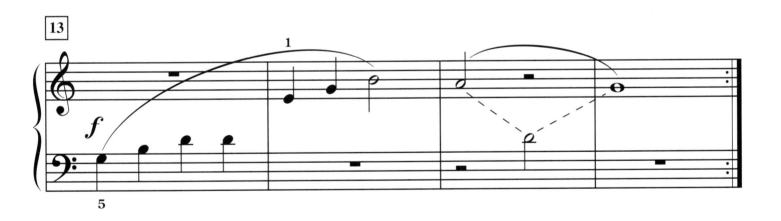

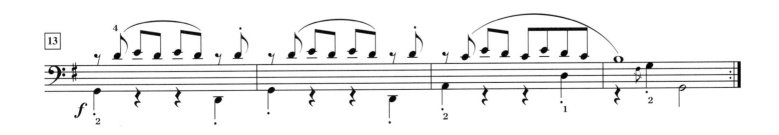

Pepperoni March

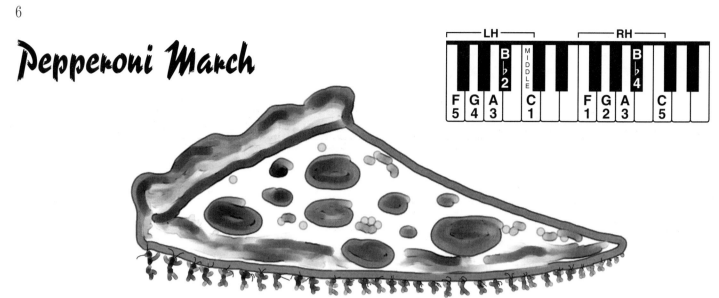

Dennis Alexander

Sturdily

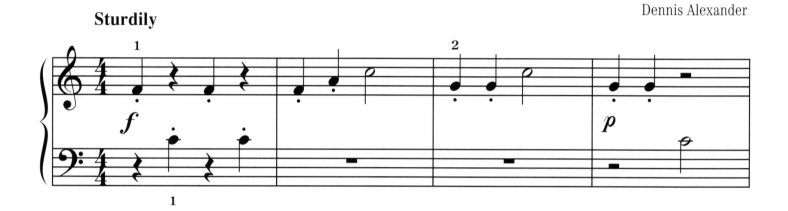

OPTIONAL DUET PART: (Student plays one octave higher.)

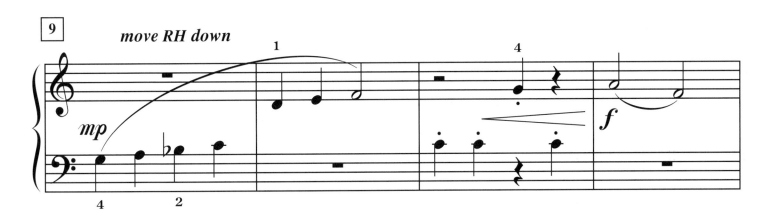

8

Hip Hop

Dennis Alexander

Merrily

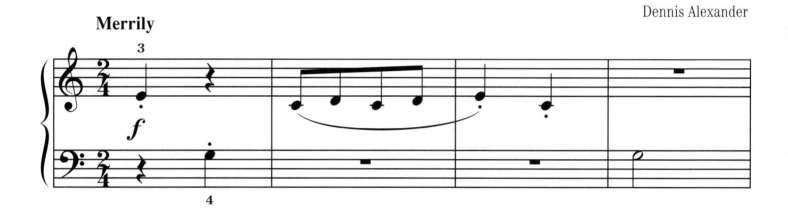

OPTIONAL DUET PART: (Student plays one octave higher.)

Merrily

Sad Warrior

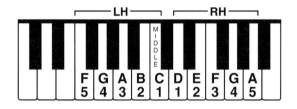

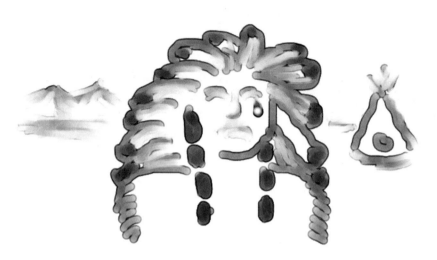

Dennis Alexander

Sadly

OPTIONAL DUET PART: (Student plays one octave higher.)

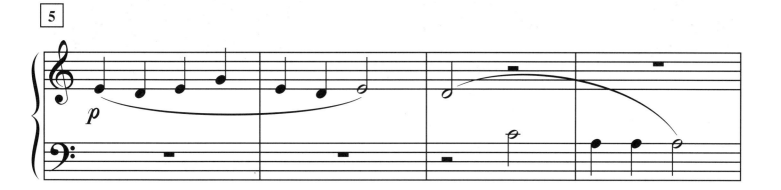

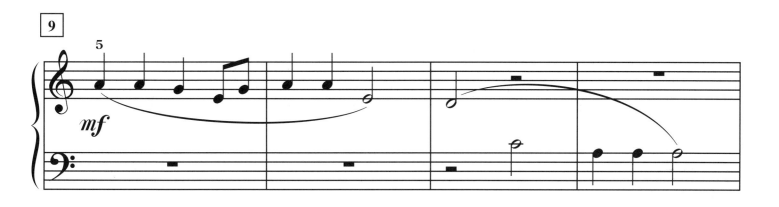

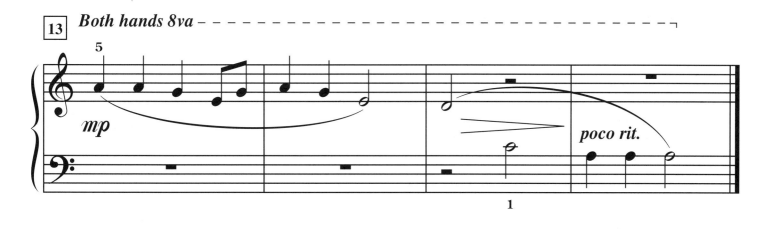

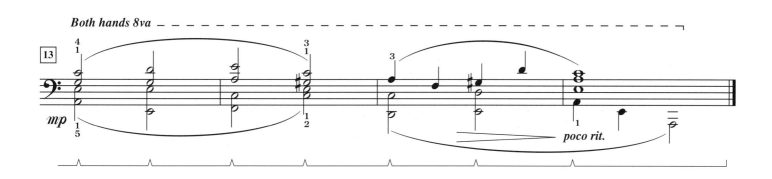

Chocolate Fudge Swirls

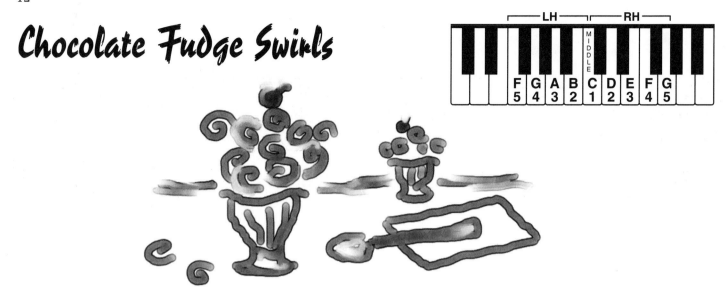

Dennis Alexander

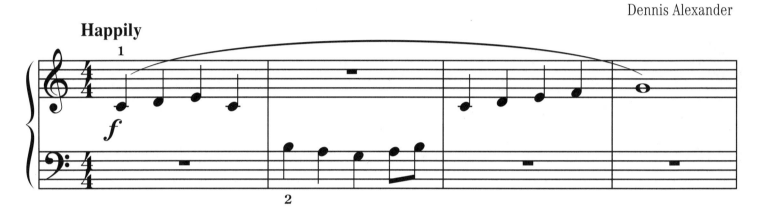

OPTIONAL DUET PART: (Student plays one octave higher.)

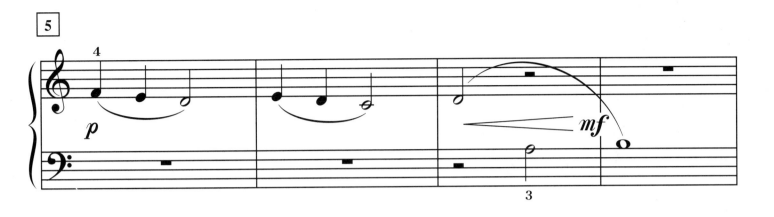

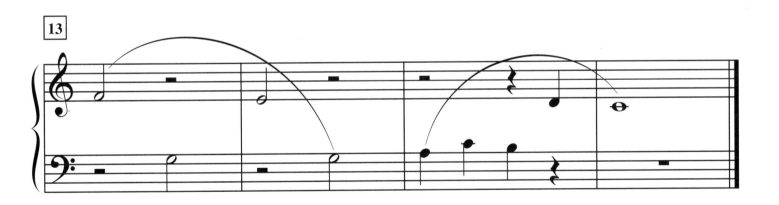

Sunday Swing

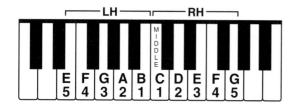

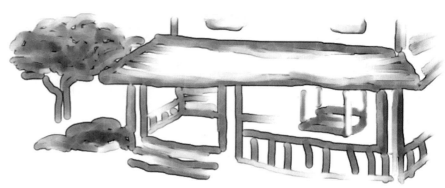

Dennis Alexander

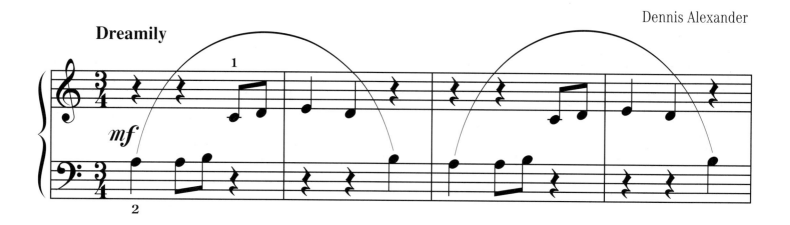

OPTIONAL DUET PART: (Student plays one octave higher.)

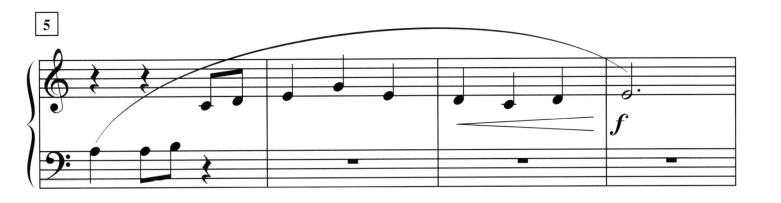

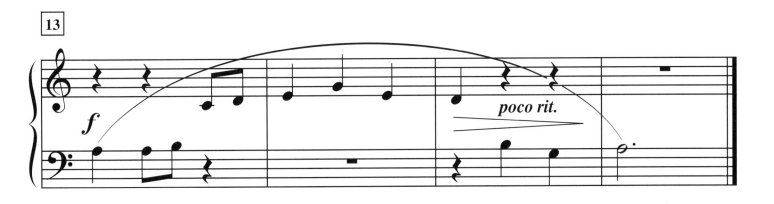

Happy Holiday!

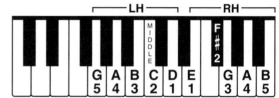

Dennis Alexander

Enthusiastically!

OPTIONAL DUET PART: (Student plays one octave higher.)

Enthusiastically!

Ancient Dance

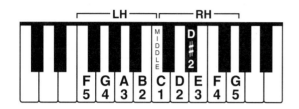

Dennis Alexander

With high energy!

OPTIONAL DUET PART: (Student plays one octave higher.)

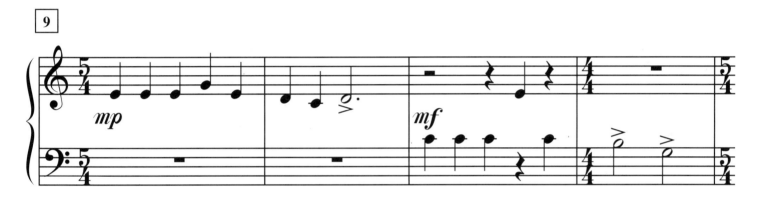

Peaceful Peach

Dennis Alexander

Tenderly

OPTIONAL DUET PART: (Student plays one octave higher.)

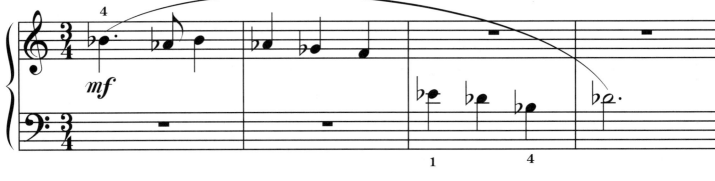

Tenderly

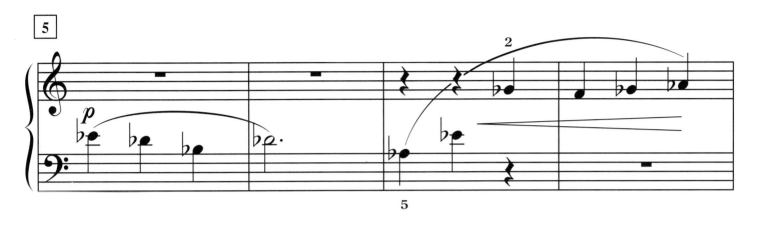

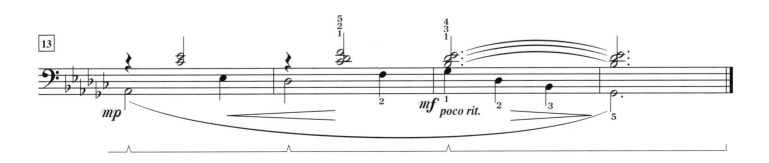

A Lazy, Hazy Day

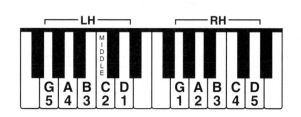

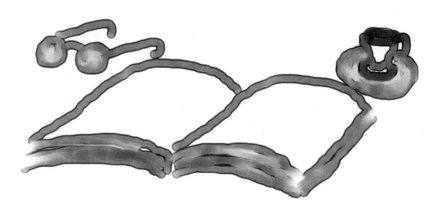

Dennis Alexander

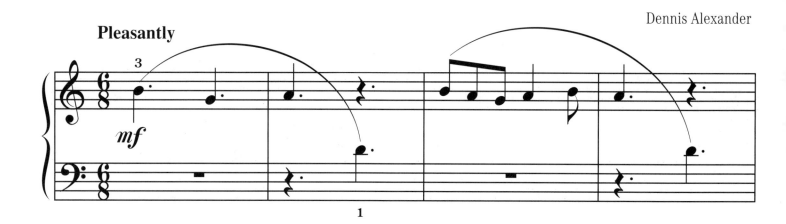

OPTIONAL DUET PART: (Student plays one octave higher.)

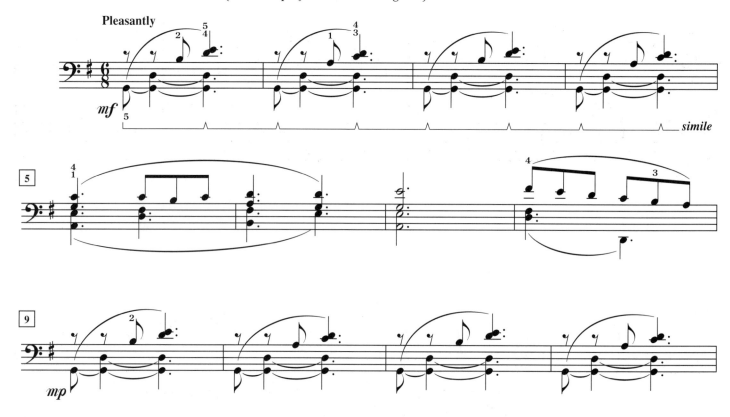

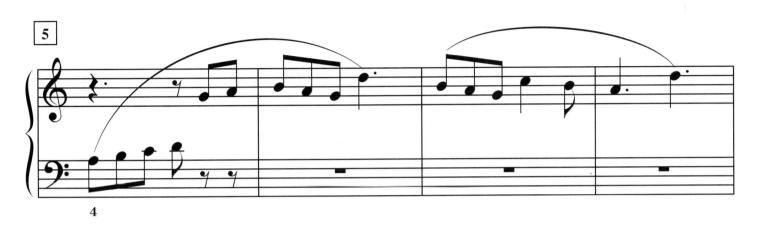

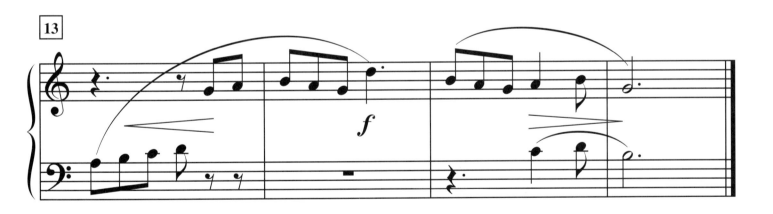

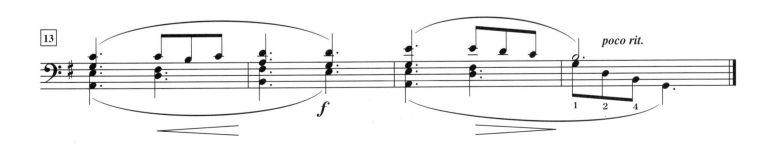